ESSAY ON ADVANTAGES & DISADVANTAGES OF NUCLEAR

Nuclear has many advantages that are good for humanity.Nuclear has served as an effiecient form energy.It releases no carbon dioxide,which contributes
to climate change.

But their are many deadly disadvantages.Terrorists can use nuclear to create weapons to wage war against other countries.If there is any earthquakes, nuclear power plants can collapse and release a lot of radiation that could harm and possibly kill thousands of people.One example is the Fukoshima nuclear power plant in Japan.During the earthquake and tsunami,it severily damaged the power plant and released radioactive fumes that contaminated the water and air around it.Countries that are prone to a lot of earthquakes shouldn't have so many nuclear power plants.They should

use renewable electricity that doesn't harm the citizens of a
certain country.

But there is only one good advantage of nuclear worth considering.It
is a form of elctricity that doesn't produce harmful greenhouse
emmisions that could harm the planet.

In conclusion,nuclear is a good source of energy that can be used in
countries that are not prone to heavy earthquakes.They should keep
nuclear away from countries that are eager to use nuclear to destroy
other countries.With that in place,nuclear will become an energy
source that many countries could use as a substitute to coal or
other energy
sources that release greenhouse gases and harm the planet.

ESSAY ON ADVANTAGES AND DISADVATAGES OF OWNING A CAR

Imagine you were on the Oregon Trail traveling to Oregon. Dust,
heat, and a long bumpy ride. Some even had to cross rivers. Then
came Henry Ford with his new invention, the Model T ford. Now people
won't have to worry about climbing mountains with difficulty,
because cars have more power than the average horse, and don't get
tired. And bridges were built, so people could get across rivers
more easily.

Until about the mid-1930s,after the Great Depression passed, and
people began to make more money and could save up enough money to
buy a car, horses were still used as a form of transportation. But
before then, only a few people in a few places could afford a car.
But gradually, wages went up, and cars became popular and cheaper,
and soon people replaced horses with cars.

Since the car was created, many people have argued whether or not it
was ok for the car to be so widely used. Car have many good effects
on on the human population, many people would say. When the car was
created in the 1910s,it was a piece of steal with a motor more
powerful than a horse, with wheels. Then in the 1930s,radios began
to appear in cars. Then, long story short, came the air
conditioning, gps, and almost all the gadgets any body in today's
technology could think of. Which is why now, people value cars more
than ever, and is why cars are so popular, because you can do more
than what you could do with a horse (although they had battery
powered radios in the time when horses were still being used, it was
too lumpy to take along, and there was nowhere to plug in the
batteries when they ran out).

But now with the recent debate of the growing issue of climate
change, it has got some people wondering, are all the good
technology that comes with the car worth it? Some say yes, some say
no, and some say I don't know. But to my opinion, I think cars could
be left where they belong, on the road, in the hands of people who
love cars. But instead of promoting gas, we should work together to
improve the new technology that we already created, like electric
cars or hydrogen cars.

Thanks to Mr.Ford,we can now get to many places faster,easier,and
more comfortable. Cars are good in many ways, and with new
technology, such as electric and hydrogen cars, we can continue to
make our transportation easier,while,in the mean time, reduce global
warming.

ESSAY ON EARTH

Earth was a giant, glowing ball of rock, about 4.6 billion years
ago. It was a totally barren place, full of lava and volcanoes. It
had no atmosphere, and it was very hot. Nothing could live there.
Then the Earth gradually cooled, until it finally rained, which
formed the oceans.

Then 240 million years ago, the dinosaurs came to rule the Earth.
Some were giant meat eaters, like the Spinosaurus and the t-rex.
Some were big plant eaters, Brachiosaurus (with long necks, like a
giraffe, except bigger). Most of the dinosaurs were in competion for
food, especially the meat eaters, because most of the meat eating
dinosaurs were predators, and they liked to keep their catch to
themselves. The herbivorous dinosaurs didn't have much
competion,they all ate leaves, so the didn't care.

After the dinosaurs went extinct, then came the crocodiles, snakes,
and other reptiles. Then came the gorillas, apes, orangutangs, and
monkeys. Then came the humans, who eventually became smarter than
the apes, and learned to make fire, use tools, and invented useful
objects.

Over the years man evolved, and became smarter, and man started to
learn new things, and eventually the life span of man gradually
increased, with the learning of new plants that could cure and heal.
Eventually disagreements sprouted among the people, and soon groups
of people broke up from other groups and eventually formed tribes,
living as they always had, hunting and farming, except they had
different philosophies.

Then man came up with a new method of hunting and fighting wars, the
rifle, invented in China around the 10th century. Cannons appeared
in Italy in 1320, then spread onward, until they finally reached the
United States in 1607 when the British set up the colony of
Jamestown, Virginia.

Then man continued to evolve. In 1910, a man named Henry Ford
created the most spectacular and beautiful thing man could ever
have, the car (although then the car was no more than just a piece
of metal, now it has all the amenities you can think of).

Finally, into present times, man continues to evolve, with new
technologies, such as the electric and hydrogen car, new and faster
internet, new tablets and phones (although these things come at a
hefty price),and many other new technologies. Mostly in today's
world, man is mostly focused on saving the planet from too much
greenhouse gas emissions so that man can continue to evolve. But if
you ask me, I think, although man has evolved into a wonderful
species, I believe that, if our efforts to save the planet work then
we should focus on the good things in
life, and stop evolving, just for a little while.

ESSAY ON E-BOOKS

E-books are the leading trend in todays technology.E-books can be
found in many places such as Amazon and Kindle.Many people now use
e-books to read their favorite books or study on their school books.

E-books are good in many ways.If somebody or someone is going on a
trip,and they are feeling bored,all they have to do is press a
botton,and they can instantly have access to millions of e-books
that you can download.Most smartphones or tablets now come with
internet access,so finding an e-book to read wouldn't be a problem.
Plus,many apps allow you to highlight a specific word so you can be
able to look up the words' meaning.And,since many regular books a
prone to being ripped,crumpled,and stained,especially on a trip,e-
books on an ipod,ipad,or smartphone will come in very handy.

But there are a few down sides as well.Many ancient history,like
history about the Roman Empire,Greek Democracy, & the Plague,can
rarely be found on an e-book,most of it is in a regular paperback
book.Also,if you are traveling on a tourist vacation to another
country that is not compatible with the networking provider on you
phone or tablet,then you're going to have some big problems with
reading your e-book,unless you have already downloaded it;though
most people who travel to Europe more likely would chat with the
people there,or take pictures of the country's landmark,such as the
Effiel Tower in Paris,France or the Colloseum in Italy.

In conclusion,e-books are good in many ways that a person can think
of,it's convenient,easy to carry,and if you have a small device such
as a smartphone,then it can also be space saving.But when it comes
to carrying it to other countries,i think we should leave the
ipods,tablets,and smartphones for another day,and explore the
massive collection of books at a European library.

ESSAY ON GLOBAL WARMING

Global warming has become a big issue for many people around the
world. Rising sea levels, melting glaciers, stronger hurricanes, and
droughts threaten everyone around the globe.

What causes global warming? Excessive burning of fossil fuels, such
as coal and gas, produce smog which act as a greenhouse gas,
trapping the sun's heat, and therefore warming the Earth.

Fossil fuels have been used for centuries. They warm our homes in
the winter, generate electricity, run our vehicles, and operate
factories. But overtime, the smog released from all this burning
creates a layer of greenhouse that traps the heat from the sun,
causing global warming.

Many people ignore the very exsistence of global warming. Either
they believe it doesn't exsist, or they simply believe that there is
no way to stop global warming, just because our daily lives rely on
fossil fuels, and there seems to be no alternative. But in reality,
global warming does exsist and is real. Fires in the Amazon
rainforest get larger, countries experience years of drought, and
hurricanes get stronger and larger.

There are many ways we can help to slow down the rate at which
global warming is happening. Recycling plastic, aluminum, metal, and
paper, will all help to slow down global warming. How? By reducing
the amount of emissions released from manufacturing companies who
make these products. Another way of reducing global warming is to
use alternative sources of energy. Renewable energy sources such as
solar power, wind power, hydroelectricity, and nuclear power will
help to reduce greenhouse gas emissions.

But these are efforts not enough if done only by one country. Large
users and manufacturers of coal, such as China and India, must also
reduce their consumption of coal and start using renewable energy.

Although there is no suitable substitutes for the gasoline powered
vehicle, new research and development on electric and hydrogen
vehicles are being done to someday reduce the use of gasoline
vehicles. We may not be able to completely eleminate the use of
gasoline or diesel powered vehicles, since they are more powerful
than hydrogen or electric cars, but we may be able to reduce its
usage until further technological advancment can be made to
eleminate the usage of gas powered vehicles for good.
In conclusion, we must do our part to help slow down global warming
by recycling, using renewable energy, and conserving energy when
appliances aren't being used. These small things in life can help
our planet live a little bit longer.

ESSAY ON GMO FOODS

A massive drought struck the Midwestern United States in the mid
1930s,worsening the case of people's lives.Farmers lost their
profits,and more families lost their property,because they couldn't
afford to pay their rent.

But then came the creation of the GMO food.These genetically
modified food can stand drought and cold.It allowed the farmers to
grow food almost anywhere and anytime without having to worry about
the crop dying.

But there are disadvantages on the usage of GMO foods.These plants
are resistant to pesticides and herbicides,and may create their own
herbicides,which may create after taste and cause health
problems.These health problems include gastrointestinal problems,and
other health problems.Plus on faulty plant can devastate the whole
crop.

In conclusion,GMO foods are good for the farmers,and make more
profits,though the scientists need to discover a way to prevent the
plants from producing their own herbicides and poisioning the
people's digestive systems.

ESSAY ON IDENTITY THEFT

With today's advancement in modern technology, identity theft is becoming a more frequent occurrence. People's money are disappearing more easily from the banks, and people are finding large sums of purchases on their credit card bill. How? Hackers can steal your passwords and other important banking information and make large purchases or steal as much as they want.

Identity theft can happen to anyone at anytime. Anyone who uses credit cards, insecure banking websites, or leaving their computer unprotected while banking can be eventually exposed and have their identity stolen. Using public computers to submit sensitive information can put you at risk for identity theft. Identity thieves can mimick important business phone calls that you are involved with to encourage you to give them important information.

In order to protect yourself from identity theft, put passwords on all your accounts, install anti-virus and anti-spy software, and, unless you have ordered something, do not answer any unknown phone calls. Shredding bills, advertisements, or receipts that could contain your important information can help prevent identity theft. Lock important documents at a safe place in your home and only take what you need when you go out. Always take your phone with you when you go out, because theives can break into your car and steal your phone. Unless you are making big purchases, don't use credit cards, pay with cash. Unless you are doing something in a hurry, don't use ATM machines, since theives can hack into ATM machines and steal your account numbers, passwords, etc. Checking your mail on a weekly can help to ensure that no one can steal your mail and your information.

In conclusion, doing these preventive precautions will not eliminate the threat of identity theft, but will help to slow down the time it will take for the identity theives to steal your identity.

ESSAY ON ADVANTAGES AND DISADVANTAGES OF ORGANIC FOOD

What is organic food? Why is organic food better than GMO (genetically modified organism) food? And what are the advantages and disadvantages of eating organic food? Well first, let us take a look into what is the definition of organic food, and what are the differences between GMO and non-GMO foods.

A non-genetically modified organism, or better known as organic food, is food that grows naturally, with no pesticides, fertilizers, or DNA alterations. Also, organic food is food that grows in it's own habitat, such as tropical fruit that grows in tropical regions.

On the other hand, a genetically modified organism, better know as GMO food, is the complete opposite. GMO foods have genetically engineered to produce their own pesticides/herbicides, to have the capability to withstand long periods of extreme weather (drought, heat, freezes), and can grow almost anywhere.

When we look at countries in Africa, the Middle East, or even several regions in Asia, where there are high levels of poverty, hunger, disease, and malnutrition, we think that there has to be a way to solve it. In 1973, biochemists Herbert Boyer and Stanley Cohen develop genetic engineering by inserting DNA from one bacteria into another. Then, in 1982 FDA approves the first consumer GMO product developed through genetic engineering: human insulin to treat diabetes.

The first GMO food product approved for usage by the FDA was in 1994. Since then, scientists genetically modified more and more crops, and soon GMO foods became more popular and widely used than organic foods. Why? Because GMO foods grow faster, can be grown anywhere, and last longer than the non-GMO version of a crop. This can be helpful in countries where poverty and starvation are high by providing more food in a faster period of time, compared to the longer growing period of a non-GMO crop.

Now that we know the history and differences of GMO and non-GMO crops, some of you may ask, "What are the disadvantages and advantages of GMO crops over non-GMO crops?" and "How should we use GMO crops?"

First and most important question, "What are the disadvantages and advantages of GMO crops over non-GMO crops?" There are many advantages to the usage of GMO crops over non-GMO crops. (1)GMO crops grow faster, therefore increasing food production and lowering prices. (2)GMO foods can grow anywhere, under any kind of weather. (3)GMO foods have longer shelf-life (the amount of time at which a product can be stored), therefore decreasing the amount of food being thrown away.

But there are also disadvantages to GMO food over non-GMO food. Genetically modified food are generally unstable, which could lead to (1) allergic reactions, (2) resistance to antibiotics, (3) immuno-suppression, (4) cancer, and (5) loss of nutrition. All of these are harmful to the human body, and could shorten the human lifespan.

Second question many people my ask is, "How should we use GMO crops?" While eating GMO foods could have some serious health consequences, GMO foods could be useful. Since GMO foods can grow anywhere at anytime, GMO foods can be grown in times of drought or other weather catastrophes to provide food in times of need. Or in times of need, where a city is recovering from a catastrophe, GMO crops can be planted to help them recover.

In conclusion, while GMO foods maybe more profitable for the farmer, it has many serious health consequences and we should find ways to adapt and consume organic food, and use GMO foods only in places or times of need.

ESSAY ON RECYCLING

Anything from aluminum to plastic to cardboard, they can all be recycled.

Anywhere from offices to schools, you see tons of cardboard or paper being thrown away. All those trees that were cut down to make those cardboards and paper were about to be sent to the wasteland. But instead, why not recycle?

Recycling cardboard and paper will have many good effects on the planet. Not so many trees will have to be cut down to make cardboards and paper, because 90% of the already used cardboards and paper will be recycled and reused. Manufacturers won't have to use so much energy to make new paper therefore reducing the amount of carbon dioxide emissions being released into the air, which will in turn decrease the greenhouse effect, which will stop the planet from heating up so quickly. Deforestation and desertification will slow down, and droughts and flash floods will not occur so frequently.

Recycling aluminum has very good advantages. It decreases the amount of energy needed to make new aluminum. Less greenhouse gases will be emitted during the manufacturing and mining process. Also many manufacturing companies that manufacture and build planes they can use aluminum to build their planes. And, also, many states offer money for every pound of aluminum you recycle.

But there could also be some serious disadvantages. Like plastic, there could also be some diseases. And aluminum cans could contain more diseases than plastic, because soda cans are usually used as drinking apparatus and are being put in the mouth. Many people with diseases drink soda or beer from aluminum cans. If the cans were not washed or sanitized before being recycled, diseases could be transmitted. Diseases like hepatitis, AIDS, or HIV. Although some stages of hepatitis have cures, AIDS and HIV don't.

Fast food chains can find this helpful. Since many states offer money for every can you recycle or every pound of aluminum cans you recycle, it can be very profitable. Almost 90% of people in fast foods and big restaurants drink sodas or beer from aluminum cans.

People can also recycle aluminum cans and aluminum trays and get a little money for their work in helping to save the planet.

Recycling plastic has many advantages. One of the most important advantages of recycling plastic is that less energy will be needed to create new plastics. Second oil refineries will release less smog into the atmosphere and decrease or slow down global warming.

But there are some disadvantages. Dirty plastics contain bacteria both from the plastic itself and the recycle bin. These bacteria pose a serious health risk to people. These bacteria include, Salmonella (from the wrapping of poultry),Ecoli (using contaminated plastic to wrap dairy meat or using contaminated plastic to hold bottled water),hepatitis, and many other diseases. Although there a some treatments for these diseases it is still not good to have them.

But there are also good advantages. Oil companies will not have to burn as much oil as they usually do when they make plastics. Less energy will be used at the plastic making companies to make more plastics. Recycling plastic is also less costly than making new plastic from new resources. Overall recycling plastics will decrease or slow down the effects of global warming.

When recycling plastics, manufacturing companies should take the following precautions.(1)Sanitize all equipment and the plastic being recycled.(2)Test the plastic if it is positive for any diseases including, Salmonella, E. coli, hepatitis, and many other diseases.(3)Require recycling companies to inspect the cleanliness of recycling bins every week.(4)Require recycling companies to inspect the delivery trucks used to deliver the plastics, and require sanitation every week.

Also recycling plastic can be profitable as well as helping to save the planet. Some states like California, Connecticut, Delaware, Hawaii, Iowa, Maine, Massachusetts, Michigan, New York, Oregon, and Vermont give $0.05 to $0.10 for each bottle water container you recycle. Although it isn't much to say as profit, you can still get rewarded for your work on helping to save the planet and reduce carbon emissions. Big fast food chains can find this especially handy because a lot of people prefer to drink bottled water rather than soda.

In conclusion, recycling has good effects on both the people and the planet, if proper precautions are not taken,(like mentioned in the plastic and aluminum) then people will suffer and so will the planet.

ESSAY ON SCHOOL UNIFORMS

Have you ever wondered why schools required children to wear
uniforms? Uniforms teaches kids discipline and to show descency.

But providing and enforcing these dress code rules at school use its
advantages and disadvantages. One of the advantages is to teach
children to be disciplined and appear well dressed in schools.

But there are some disadvantages to using uniforms. Providing school
uniforms can be costly. Also requiring children at school to wear
their uniforms puts pressure on the kids and makes them stressed out
because they cant wear their usual normal everyday clothes. Some
kids might show up late at school just because they don't want to
wear their uniform.

An effective way to solve this problem is to issue specific days
when to use their uniform and when not to. That way, schools won't
have to buy uniforms for everyday of the month, and it will also
give children a chance to alternate their uniforms with their normal
everyday clothes. School uniforms should only be required to be used
only half the week, Monday to Tuesday,and the rest of the days
Wednesday to Friday, they should be allowed to wear the clothes of
their choice. It shouldn't be mandatory to must wear their usual
clothes on the days of Wednesday to Friday,but it also doesn't mean
they must wear their uniforms either. In other words Monday to
Tuesday they must wear their uniforms,but on the days of Thursday to
Friday they have the choice of either to wear their uniforms or to
wear their normal everyday clothes.

In conclusion, wearing school uniforms can provide kids the
opportunity to look disciplined and well dressed in front of the
class, they should be given the chance to have a few days to have a
choice of their own whether they want of don't want to wear their
school uniform. Plus schools won't have to spend so much money to
provide the uniforms, and to replace them if they got ripped.

ESSAY ON TEAMWORK
Teamwork is good in many ways. Teamwork gives people the opportunity
to make friends. It helps to get work done faster.

Teams must be disciplined and have a good leader. Teams must be well
trained in a specific work force. Teams help people to learn from
each other. It is very motivating for people to become part of
something that give them recognition and where their worth is
acknowledged. In doing so, they could get a promotion, until
eventually the become a team leader.

But teams have some disadvantages. Disagreements among team members
can lead to fights, in which a person can take his or her own
friends and form their team, therefore disrupting the workforce.

In conclusion, for teams to be effective, they must have a good
leader, good training and discipline. Without these three important
qualifications, teams are most likely to fight among themselves,
leading to an inefficient team, which will more likely lead to
people leaving to form their own teams, disrupting the workforce.

ESSAY ON THE ADVANTAGES AND DISADVANTAGES OF HAVING PHYSICAL ED. IN
SCHOOL

Ever saw kids running around on the school grounds,which has you
wondering,is school over? Many schools enforce physical education
during recess hours or before lunch. It helps to prevent obesity,
which has become a major problem among kids. Plus it helps to keep
kids active,and gives them the opportunity to make friends.

But is physical education really worth it? Many kids get tired waking up at 7:00 in the morning, and having to sometimes walk to school, is just tiring for many kids. And physical education just makes them more tired, and soon they lose focus, and can't wait till school is over to get home and get some sleep. Also lack of sleep and other kids pestering you to play basketball or soccer just makes you angry and, if you take your anger out on your friends, you're likely to lose them. So, is physical education really worth the time? Let's discuss the advantages and disadvantages of physical education.

Like mentioned above, obesity has become a major problem among many Americans. Many Americans have a burrito or taco or some other Mexican food, that they end up in the hospital, trying to lose that weight, which cost lots of money. Now many kids grow up eating Mexican food and end up becoming fat before they even reach past age 5. Now tell me that's not obesity. So physical education give children a chance to lose some of that weight, although, if they have more Mexican food for dinner, then they end up gaining the weight back. So physical education in school is still a good thing since it helps kids to lose some weight, even though they still end up obese in their old age, it prevents them from become obese too soon in their young age.

But, there are also some disadvantages. Like mentioned above, kids are already under the stress of waking up early, walking to school, and then walking back from school, then doing their homework, it might be a little too much stress for the kids to take all at one time. Some kids just don't have the energy to do all that stuff in one day. Another disadvantage is that schools also need funds to keep the school's play spaces clean, keep the lawn clipped and watered, and make sure that the basketball courts and soccer pens are in good condition.

So, is enforcing the term physical education in schools are good or bad thing?In opinion, I believe that the kids from ages 15 - the age that they graduate (18 or 21), should be given a choice whether or not they want to participate in physical education. But for younger kids, they must participate in physical education, to ensure that the rate at which they become obese slows down. I don't believe that physical education should be used as a method to get rid of obesity once and for all, but I do believe we can slow it down. Also they should minimize how much soda and other soft drinks that they serve in schools, so that children can regenerate their lost energy, but minimizes it enough so that they don't gain their weight back.

In conclusion, physical education should not be made mandatory for all kids, but younger must participate in physical education, to ensure that
the rate of obesity is slowed down.

ESSAY ON THE ADVANTAGES AND DISADVANTAGES OF HAVING POLICE

Since the colonization of the the thirteen colonies in America,
there were always something to keep the peace and enforce the laws.
During the days of the colonization, soldiers patrolled the streets,
enforcing the laws, and keep the peace among the people. Anyone who
disobeyed the king, or mocked the king at the worst case, then the
soldiers would come and drag them to the king.

Then the American Revolution came. Soldiers still patrolled the
streets, until a few years after the war of 1812,in 1829.Then
soldiers duties became the role that the soldiers play today,
defending and protecting the freedom and rights of the American
people, and providing supplies in times of disaster, on American
soil, and our allies.

But now, with the formation of gangs and other criminal groups,
police's lives are endangered in almost every riot and protest.
Which got many people thinking: is it really wise to have police
endanger their lives? Well, having the police has many advantages
and disadvantages. One of the advantages of the police is safety of
the people. Police patrol communities and schools, and if there is a
public gathering, like a Thanksgiving, Christmas, or New Years party
at a local school, police help to maintain the peace, enforce the
laws, and keep people safe. Also police help to keep roads closed
during a wildfire, which has happened many times, and police also
patrol the roads within their assigned jurisdiction, stopping
speeders and helping during accidents.

But it also has disadvantages. State has to provided updated
equipment and good salary for the police, which means more tax money
has to come from the people. More people means more police, and more
police usually leads to tax increases to fund the influx of police
required to keep the people safe. Also in big cities such Los
Angeles, San Francisco, Chicago, New York City, and Manhattan, riots
tend to occur almost on an everyday basis. Why? Many people believe
that the people and citizens of the country and state are capable of
defending themselves, and that police hog up so much tax money that
could be better spent on welfare for the people, and providing

services for the poor and homeless. But think. If there were to be a
city with no police, and the mayor of that city created new laws,
who would enforce them? The people cannot go around and knocking
other people's doors and tell them about the new laws, and further
more, even if you could do that, what are the chances that they
would follow it? With no police to enforce the new law, people would
think that it was just another sentence, written on a piece of
paper.

So, is it really beneficial to have the police? In my opinion, yes.
Police help to enforce the laws, new ones and old ones, past and
future. Police help to ensure that the people follow them, they
ensure that the people rights are protected, they keep the peace,
and protect the people. Police should be honored and respected by
the people. And if anyone complains that police hog up tax money,
and that the state isn't doing enough to give welfare and provide
for the homeless, I'm pretty sure that the government can help with
that.

ESSAY ON THE ADVANTAGES AND DISADVANTAGES OF OWNING A CAR

Since the English people came and made the first colony in America,
people have been using horses to go to work, market, or to plow the
field. Horses were the hardworking animals people used for almost
everything in everyday life.

But horses posed a series of problem. Horses needed shoes, for the
horses feet, or the horses feet would be too painful to walk on.
When climbing mountains, horses didn't have the right amount of
power to go up the steep slopes, since many poor people couldn't
afford no more then one or two horses.

Then came Henry Ford, the inventor of the car. Cars came with more power than the average horse, so cars were a lot better than horses. But not many people decided that cars were more better than horses. Plus, many of the middle class, hardworking Americans couldn't afford the price of a new car, straight from the assembly line.

Then gradually,more and more people got hired to work for Mr.Ford, and cars were soon made faster, which allowed for the prices to gradually go down, but they didn't go down overnight. Soon, by the mid-1900s,cars became a common sight on many roads, and many horses were soon used just on the family farm since tractors weren't around yet to plow the land.

But now, every American has a car. Cars have their advantages and disadvantages. Cars during the mid-1900s didn't have the technology that we have today, so cars today are a lot better than the cars of that time. Cars today have more power to get you over hills and mountains, and now cars come with gps, radio, charging ports for you phone (although there weren't any phones in the 1900s that you could carry with you on a trip).

But cars also have their disadvantages. Cars today have more power, so they also release more greenhouse gas emissions,which contributes to the acceleration of global warming. Even though with the newly created electric car,which has yet to improve, people still have to use gas cars while waiting for electric cars to improve. Also,since cars have more power, and come with more gadgets, they are also becoming more expensive for people to afford.

In conclusion, cars are good, especially with the new technology. But,in my opinion, cars are powerful and heavy duty enough for the satisfaction of many people. Car manufacturing companies should focus on improving electric car technology, so that people can buy electric cars to reduce green house gas emissions.

ESSAY ON OWNING A DOG

Dogs are cute and beautiful creatures. Whether big or small, dogs
are good partners for family life.

Dogs have many good advantages for many people, families and
disabled. Dogs help to keep people and families company. Having a
dog also gives you the opportunity to go out and get some exercise,
because dogs also must take a walk at least once a day. Dogs also
help you to relax, because at least there is one happy face to look
at. Also dogs help the blind people to guide them and guard them.

Since there are many good advantages worth considering when wanting
to own a dog, there are many different kinds of dog breeds that you
might and might not want to have. If you want to have a friend,
someone who is loyal to you and like to play big dogs such as Golden
retrievers and puddles would be a good choice. But if you want to
have a loyal dog who can bite when it sees an intruder, but is also
friendly when it sees you, and gives you comfort, then perhaps a dog
like German shepherd would be a good choice.

But dogs have their disadvantages. When it comes to owning a dog,
they need food and must have exercise. Also even if they are
healthy, they must still go to the vet at least once a year. Also
you must have time to give them a bath and take them on walks. Also
you have to clean up after them when they have to their business on
the street. Also when you travel, you must find an airline that will
allow you to take the pet with you, and you must also find a hotel
that will allow you to stay there until you are finished with the
vacation. Also you must find restaurants that will serve you if you
have pet.

Altogether, in conclusion, if you want a friend, someone to keep you
company, and guard you when you sleep, then dogs are good. But if
you are constantly a busy person, and might not have time to care
for dog, then you might not want have a dog.

ESSAY ON ADVANTAGES AND DISADVANTAGES OF THE ELECTRIC CAR

The gasoline powered vehicle first came out in Germany in January
29, 1886 by Carl Benz. Then came Henry Ford's first publicized
version of the gas powered car, in 1908 with the creation of the
Model T which was soon mass produced and many Americans by the 1920s
had learned to drive the Model T.

As the car industry progressed, engineers began researching ways to reduce the greenhouse gas emissions, while still providing for the luxury, comfort, and speed of the normal car:the electric car. Although the first prototype of the electric car came out and was publicly tested in 1890, and went a speed of 14 miles per hr., it was not widely acknowledged because of the inefficiency of the batteries constantly running out power. So the idea of the electric car died out,and the gas powered engine rose to popularity.

As the years progressed, and as technology progressed, engineers began researching the electric car, again. This time they were more successful, and mass produced,but not many people rushed to buy it, and therefore not sold everywhere, and weren't very popular.

Now that the technology was produced, tested, and sold, many politicians pushed to get car dealers to mass produce, sell and replace all gasoline powered vehicles to electric cars, because of the less noise, and less or no greenhouse gases to be released into the air, therefore reducing air polution and smog, which therefore increases the air quality.

But the electric car has a few advantages and disadvantages. One of the main advantages is that fossil fuels is in limited supply, and electric cars don't use gas, which reduces the amount of fossil fuels used. Many cars also come equiped with recyclable batteries, which will not cause a disposal problem.

But there are also many disadvantages. One is refuelling or recharging. A gas car take about 1-2 minutes max while a electric car can take up to 10 hours to charge, which means that if you run low on charge, you won't be able to to just plug in charge and go. The only way to get sufficient charge is to plug overnight. Second disadvantage is distance. An fully charged electric car will take you to a distance of 50 to 120 miles before needing to recharge. A normal gas powered vehicle an get you about twice as far, and gas stations are also widely available. Third is places to charge.Although there are many charging stations available, many would prefer to charge at home, which you would a converter. And finally, the fourth disadvantage is power supply. Everyone here talks about electric cars being ecofriendly, none polluting vehicles. But one fact that many of the promoters of the electric car usually ignore, or just don't want the people to know about, is that the electric car runs on electricity, which comes from power stations, that still use fossil fuels! (although some power stations use hydroelectricity or solar,majority of powerplants still use fossil fuels.)

In conclusion, the question that is still hanging in the air: Are electric cars really worth the switch? Should we really get rid of all our gas powered vehicles and move on to electric cars? The answer:No. Electric cars are not efficient as everyone think, and electric cars will never gain the attention of the public (unless they are the last thing on the market.) Gas powered vehicles are still more efficient, and more powerful than electric cars, and many

people who do construction work, semi-trucking, camper towing, and
even racing, will want to keep their powerful gas engines running
for many years to come.

ESSAY ON VACCINES

A vaccination is a procedure that protects people against a
particular disease. Vaccinations are usually given as injections (or
shots) through the skin with a needle. Other vaccinations are given
by mouth. You may remember receiving vaccinations when you were a
young child.

The first modern vaccination was developed by Edward Jenner, who was
an English country doctor. Jenner noticed that people who had been
in contact with cowpox, a mild viral disease usually affecting cows,
never got smallpox, which is a more serious and often fatal disease.
Jenner had the idea that a person might be given cowpox in order to
protect him from smallpox. A young boy was Jenner's first patient.
Jenner injected the boy with the cowpox, or vaccinia, virus. The boy
did not contract smallpox- and neither did others tested later.
That's how the smallpox vaccine was born.

Although Jenner himself did not understand how vaccines work, we now
know that vaccinations work because they stimulate the body's immune
system to build antibodies that protect the body against infections.

The term vaccination originally meant injection with the vaccinia
(cowpox virus). But today, getting a vaccination can offer us
protection from many diseases that are frequently fatal to many
people. There are now vaccines that protect us from tetanus, flu,
polio, rabies, and soon COVID-19.

Although scientists continue to study the body's immune system and
develop new vaccines, there are still a number of viral disease that
still do not have any vaccines available. The AIDS (Acquired Immune
Deficiency Syndrome) disease and HIV are examples. AIDS is a deadly
viral disease that has become a serious health problem in recent
years. The AIDS virus attacks the immune system and makes it
difficult and sometimes impossible, for a person to resist and fight
off other diseases. People with AIDS become very susceptible to
infections.

In many parts of the world, AIDS has reached epidemic proportions. Some scientists estimate that as many as 40 million people may already have this disease. Although there is no cure for AIDS the disease can be treated and sometimes held at bay using expensive medicines.

There are 10 reasons why you and your family should get vaccinated. You should vaccinate your children to make sure they are healthy and protected from illnesses, is on reason. Two, vaccination protection protects children from diseases that cause amputation, paralysis of limbs, hearing loss, convulsions, brain damage, and death. Three, measles, mumps, and whooping cough disease are still a threat. Four, vaccinations leads to a decline in the number of U.S cases of infectious disease. Five, outbreaks of preventable disease occur when parents do not vaccinate their children. Six, vaccinations are safe and effective. Seven, organizations like the CDC support vaccinating children. Eight, vaccination protects children and others you care about, including other family members, friends, and relatives. Nine, if you don't get vaccinated and people with weakened immune systems get sick, can result in death. And lastly, number ten, all people have a health commitment to protect each other's children by vaccinating our family members.

Although vaccines are safe, it is all very important to monitor vaccine safety. Once a vaccination is used, it is continually monitored for safety and efficacy. Vaccines, like any medication, can have adverse effects. A decision not to immunize a child involves risk. If you don't immunize your child, you are facing a decision of either putting the child at risk of contracting a disease that could be dangerous or deadly.

After you immunize your child, he or she will experience mild side effects. Some of them could include redness and swelling where the shot was given, which can be cured by using cool wet cloth. Other side effects, will include redness, soreness, and swelling. But these are just the mild side effects. There are some serious side effects that include severe allergic reaction. But do not worry. These side effects rarely occur. If your child experiences a severe allergic reaction after the vaccination was given, take him or her to the doctor. Doctors and clinic staff are trained to deal with them.

In conclusion, vaccines are safe effective and help to protect children, relatives, friends, and other people that you care about.

ESSAY ON THE DIGESTIVE SYSTEM

The digestive system is a complex bodily function that some people
may not understand. This essay will cover some of the basic
functions of the digestive system as well as how the digestive
system works.

The digestive system consists of: the mouth, esophagus, stomach,
liver, small intestine and large intestine. The digestive system
begins first with the mouth. The mouth is considered one of the most
important organs in the body, next to the stomach. Why? Because
without the mouth, food would be unable to pass through the
esophagus to the stomach. The mouth plays a major role in the
digestive system by chewing (or processing) large chunks of food and
mixing it with an acidic chemical known as saliva to create a bolus
(a small ball of softened food). The tongue helps in this process,
by moving the food around in the mouth to properly chew the food.
The tongue then helps to push the food to the back of the mouth to
the esophagus, where it will begin its journey to the stomach.

The next major organ in the digestive system is the stomach. The
stomach is a large thick muscle full of acid. Think of the stomach
as a large tub of acid. As soon as the food enters the stomach,
acids and enzymes in the stomach begin to break down the proteins,
carbohydrates, fats, and other nutrients in the food you have eaten.
It prepares it for passage to the small intestine, where it will
begin further processing, along with absorption into the
bloodstream.

The liver plays little part in the role of digestive system but it
does have several functions. Bile from the liver is secreted into
the small intestine and the liver also processes some vitmans that
are absorbed from the food to help keep your body healthy.

The food then moves to the small intestine, where further processing
is done. The small intestine begins the absorption of nutrients into
the bloodstream, and it also begins the process of removing
undigested food sending to the large intestine where it will then be
excreted from the body.

The final step in the process of the digestive system is the arrival
of food at the large intestine, where the undigested food particles
undergo dehydration, since the large intestine absorbs water and
salt from the undigested food (which explains dry stool). The large
intestine also helps produce Vitamin K.

So now that we know how th digestive works, and its basic functions,
what can go wrong with the digestive system? The digestive system is
prone to many problems including stomach ulcer, liver cancer, and
colon cancer, just to name a few of the most serious digestive
system malfunctions. Stomach ulcer is caused by unhealthy or uneven
eating habits caused by job stress, illness, or skipping meals. Acid
in the stomach begins to deteriorate the inner linning of the
stomach, causing pain. Liver cancer, another major problem with the
digestive system, is caused by too much alcoholic beverages and
smoking. Failure of the liver can cause the body to lose nutrient
absorption and can also cause the body to lose red blood cells and
become anemic, since the liver is a major producer of red blood
cells. Liver failure will usually require medication or a liver
transplant to restore the body's functions. Colon cancer, another
major problem of the digestive system, is caused by irregular bowel
movement, due to irregular eating habits, large consumptions of
carbohydrates, a lack of a fiber enhanced diet, and a lack of
fluids. Medication such as laxative is usually required.

In conclusion, keeping a healthy digestive system is important, to
help avoid future problems such as anemia, colon cancer, and liver
cancer. Elderly people should continue to maintain there regular
eating habits, since they are more susceptible to digestive
failures. Regular physical examinations can help detect a serious
digestive problem before they occur, and can help you treat it
before it gets worst.

ESSAY ON HOW TALENT IS ESSENTIAL TO SUCCESS

In this era, all people wish succeed in life to fulfill their needs.
There are solutions to obtain success in life. Some people who have

natural talent, while others are working to be good in personality.
As you read this essay you will learn more about the importance of
hard work and talent as the key to success.

Some people believe that one of the keys to succeed in life is hard
work. Firstly, someone who works hard will definitely get a lot of
experience and skill which can help people get a better job. Good
relationships can also help a person get a promotion in their life.
For example, a doctor who has no talent can become a doctor when
they work harder, because people who work hard have good results. So
working hard can help obtain success in a person's life, because of
the experience, skill, and relationship that they have.

On the other hand, some people believe that having talent is a
better ability that can help a person to get success in life.
Generally, people who have talent have the ability to easily learn
anything, and can help a person achieve their goal to get what they
want. With talent, people can achieve what they want in accordance
with expertise. But talent does not always help who to get success
in life because talent must have the desirability and plan to
succeed.

So, which is better? Well, hard work is more important than having
talent, because sometimes people who have talent are not always
accepted in a society. Besides, talented people should also work
hard to prove that he or she is actually talented for a specific
job. It is hard to find someone with unique skills or abilities, so
having a unique talent opens a lot of opportunities for the person
that has it. Most people who have a unique talent of skill believe
that they do not need to work as hard as others, but there is always
a need for hard work, no matter how talented you may be. A lot of
people want someone who knows how to use a unique skill. It does not
matter if you have any talent at all, someone who has the ability to
work hard can beat a person with talent. If a person with talent
works hard, then the talent can go above and beyond its capabilities
that not even a hard worker can do.

In conclusion, talent and hard work can go together to help a person
achieve success, but hard work can also help lead a person to
success, because makes perfect.

ESSAY ON ANTIBIOTICS

What is an antibiotic? The word antibiotic is used to describe a
drug that is produced by certain microbes. Most doctors use
antibiotics to help fight genes in a patient. Antibiotics can be
obtained from plants, fungi, air, water, soil, just about anything
on Earth. Antibiotics can kill and attack the germs and virus in the
body, but they do not hurt the human cells, ordinarilly.

Antibiotics are used to treat many various types of diseases, such
as Tuberculosis, syphilis, and several other kinds of infections.
People have been using antibiotics for more than 2500 years. They
used molds to help cure some skin infections and rashes.

In the late 1800s the real study of medicine began. Louis Pasteur
discovered that the bacterium was responsible for the cause of
disease, and proved wrong the theory of spontaneous generation.
After him came a man named Robert Koch, who developed a method of
isolating and growing bacteria. Scientists tried to develop a drug
that could kill microbes, but they proved to be either too dangerous
or ineffective.

In 1928, there was a discovery by a man named Alexander Fleming. He
detected that a substance that he called "penicillin" could destroy
the bacteria. Then in the late 1930s, two British scientists
invented a method of extracting penicillin from the mold. This was
the start of developing new drugs to treat disease and bacteria.

Over the years, numerous thousands of antibiotic material have been
found in nature, as well as produced chemically, but, they are only
a few antibiotics that are safe and useful. However, the ones that
are safe and useful have saved many lives and have helped to extend
life expectancy. Right now there are more than 70 different kinds of
antibiotics in use. Most antibiotics are used to treat infections,
some are used for fungi protozoa, but antibiotics are not usually

effective against viruses. So they have developed other methods such
as vaccines to fight viruses.

How do antibiotics work? There are three ways antibiotics work. One,
they prevent the cell from growing, two, obstruct the cell membrane,
or three disrupt the chemical process. When the antibiotic prevents
the cell wall from growing, the antitoxin surrounds the bacteria's
membrane, and then it forms a rigid wall that stops the cell wall
from spliting open, which would producing another cell. The human
cells are not affected by this because human cells do not have cell
wall. If the antibiotic obstruct the cell membranes, which control
the flow of items in and out of the cell, the essential nourishment
can escape the cell. Then a toxic substance can enter the cell,
killing it. Human cells are not affected by this method because the
antitoxin only affects the microbial cells. If the antitoxin
disrupts the chemical process then the microbe cannot survive. The
cells need the proteins and nucleic acids that they produced to
survive, and by interfering with this process, the cell cannot
survive. Human cells are immune to this method because, both kinds
of cells produce proteins and acids to survive, but the methods of
making the proteins in each cell differ enough for the antibiotic to
decipher the different methods.

Antibiotics are the safest kinds of drugs when properly used, but
misuse could lead to dangerous side effects, or even death. There
are three main dangerous reactions that could happen with the misuse
of antibiotics: (1) allergic reactions, (2) eradication of good
microbes, and (3) damage to organs and tissues. Although most
allergic reactions are not that severe, if a person is highly
allergic to what they were exposed to, they could die. Every
antibiotic made could produce an allergic reaction, but the most
common is penicillin. Approximately 10% of people in the United
States have an allergic reaction to penicillin.

In conclusion, if used properly, antibiotics can be very helpful to
the human body, but if used improperly, can led to serious
consequences.

ESSAY ON THE THYROID GLAND

What is the thyroid gland? The thyroid gland is an endocrine gland
that consist of two connected lobes. They are connected by a band of
tissue called the thyroid isthmus. The thyroid gland is located in
front of the neck, just below the Adams apple.

What is the structure of the thyroid gland? The thyroid gland is a
butterfly shaped organ consisted of two lobes, the left and the

right, connected by an isthmus. The thyroid gland typically weighs
25 grams in adults, and each lobe is usually 5 cm long, 3 cm wide, 2
cm thick, and the isthmus 1.25 cm in height and width. The gland is
larger in women than in men, and increases in size during pregnancy.
The thyroid gland is supplied with blood from superior thyroid
artery, which is a branch of the external carotid artery, and the
inferior thyroid artery, which is a branch of the thyrocervical
trunk. The thyroid gland receives sympathetic nerve supply from the
superior, middle, and inferior cervical ganglion of the sympathetic
trunk. The thyroid gland receives parasympathetic nerve supply from
the superior laryngeal nerve and the recurrent laryngeal nerve.

What are the functions of the thyroid gland? The main function of
the thyroid gland is to produce iodine-containing thyroid hormones,
triiodothyronine (T3) and thyroxine (T4) and the peptide hormone
calcitonin. These hormones have a wide range of effects on the human
body which include:

Metabolic: thyroid hormones help increase basal metabolic rate,
which have effects on almost all body tissues. Appetite, and the
absorption nutrients, are all influenced by thyroid hormones.
Thyroid hormones increase absorption in the gut, uptake in the
cells, and breakdown of glucose. They also help in the breakdown of
fats, and increase the amount of free fatty acids. Although the
number of free fatty acids increases, the thyroid hormones reduce
cholesterol levels, by increasing the rate of cholesterol secretion
in bile.

Cardiovascular: the thyroid hormones help increase the rate and
strength of heartbeat. They also help increase the rate of
breathing, intake and consumption of oxygen, and increase activity
of mitochondria. Combining these help increase the body's blood flow
and temperature.

Development: the thyroid hormones help in development by increasing
the growth rate in younger people. Thyroid hormones also aid in
brain maturation during fetal development and the first few years of
postnatal life.

How are thyroid hormones produced? Thyroid hormones are produced by
thryoglobin, which is a protein within the colloid in the follicular
lumen that is originally created within the rough endoplasmic
reticulum of follicular cells and then transported into the
follicular lumen. Thyroglobin contains units of tyrosine, which
reacts with iodine within follicular lumen.

What are the dysfuntions of the of the thyroid gland?
Hyperthyroidism, hypothyroidism, Graves disease, Goitre,
Thyroiditis, and thyroid cancer one of the few common types of
thyroid dysfunctions. Iodine deficiency can lead to goitre, known as
endemic goitre. Pregenant women with iodine deficiency can give
birth to children with thyroid hormone deficiency.

In conclusion, maintaining a healthy diet and checking hormone
levels through blood tests, can help prevent harmful diseases to the
thyroid.

ESSAY IN VIRAL AND BACTERIAL DISEASES

Bacteria constitute of a unique group of one-celled organisms.
During the last few decades, much has been known on the structure of
reproduction and the importance of bacteria. The organism has become
a prolific source (and importance of bacteria) of research of
biologists, biotechnologies, microbiologists, chemists, and medical
professionals. Common man is influence by the organism in many ways.

Where do bacteria occur? Bacteria are ubiquitos in nature. They are
among the most numerous of the living beings present in all
conceivable environments. They are present in aquatic habitats.
Every moment we breathe in or breathe out a number of bacteria that
are present in everything we eat. They can thrive in all parts of
our body, right from the mouth parts to the terminal part of the
digestive system. They can withstand extreme conditions of
temperature. Bacteria are being detected from hot springs, saline
waters, and from the tops of icy mountains. They are also found in
huge numbers from all types of soils. The reasons for their
universal distribution are: highly simple structure. Faster
metabolism under suitable conditions. Resistance of the vegetable
cells to adverse environmental conditions. Formation of heat
resistant endospores. Diversity of the mode of nutrition.

Bacteria come in all shapes and sizes. Not all bacteria are visible
to the naked eye. They can only be seen under the microscope.
Dimension of bacteria are measured in microns. The bacteria are much
variable in their shape. They ordinally occur in many forms-rods,
spheres, and helices. Again, under these, there are types of
bacteria that may be cylindrical, straight, or slightly curved with
rounded or blunt ends. These are called bacillus forms or baccili.
These forms of bacteria are common and range from diameter and
length. Some are flagellated also. The bacilli may occur singly or
in groups of twos (diplibacillus). When bacilli occurs in chains, we
call it streptobacillus. Occassionally, bacilli may occur in
parallel or palisade arrangement. Spherical bacteria, this group of
bacteria with spherical or ellipsoidal cells vary from 0.5 to 1.25
micron in diameter. These are called coccal forms or cocci. Almost
all coccal bacteria are not flagellated. These forms may occur

singly. But when they occur in twos, fours, and in chains are
respectively called diplococcus, tetracoccus, and streptococcus. The
coccal bacteria may occur in loose masses of variable size and
irregular in shape which are called staphylococci. Helical bacteria,
bacteria cells twisted spirally with 1 to 5 complete turns are
called spirilla. When bacteria cell is short and looks like a curved
rod are called vibrios. Vibrosis have flagella at one pole only.
Filament forms when bacterial cells divide and join to one another.
The number of filamentous forms are very rare.

In conclusion, bacteria can be found anywhere at anytime, and can
come in many shapes and sizes.

ESSAY ON HOW COLLEGES SHOULD FOCUS ON TEACHING REAL WORLD JOB SKILLS

If students are going to make a successful transition to college and
career, schools need to do more than focus on academic studies.
Experts say helping students develop self-discipline and critical
thinking needs to be prioritized as well. A new report by the New
America Foundation emphasizes the value of these "skills for
success" and encourages K-12 educators to integrate activities to
promote them in the classroom. While prekindergarten programs have
paid attention to this holistic approach to teaching that focus is
often lost in elementary, middle, and high school, according to
"skills for Success Supporting and Assessing key Habits, Mindsets,
and Skills in Pre-K-12" released last week. The report makes several
recommendations for how government, local, education agencies, and
research institutions can encourage schools to devote time to
developing these life skills. Schools should make practices that

influence students students skills in the areas more visible and progress should be monitored by outside stakeholders. This should not be at the expense of moving away from accountability for academic achievment. For these skills to receive attention, educators need to understand their value and learn about strategies for promoting them through training.

There are some promising approaches available, both from Pre-K and K-12, for supporting the skills, habits, and mindsets that enable students to be successful academically as well as professionally and personally throughout their lives. The New America Foundation recommends funding more research to find out the most effective approaches to teaching these life skills and establishing regulations to create skills for success standards that can help ensure schools make this a priority. College has always been thought of as the key into the world of work. High corporate jobs look for a college education because they know that you have the experience to work.

However, in reality that is not the case. When it comes to prepare students for the world of work, it is not the colleges primary function because it is really the experiences outside of college that prepare you the most. Many people think that college teaches you to work in the real world. Yet, when you really look at the situation carefully, it is easy to see that experiences that you encounter outside of school are the things that shape you for the working world.

Internships are specially designed to prepare you how to succeed once you get a job. Without internships, it would be extremely difficult for a newly graduated college student to get out in the working world and try to be successful. The only thing that the student would have with them is the knowledge-but that student would not have any clue in how to use that knowledge. Basically his or her time in college would be a complete waste of time. Colleges are made for you to spend two or more years focusing on information that you are not really going to need for your major. These classes that students spend half of their college career on is called General Education (G.E.). G.E. is required for students to take in order for them to move on and take classes that focus primarilly on their major. As much as students and teachers agree that General Education is a waste time, colleges still force students to take G.E courses.

In conclusion, is college really worth the time and money wasted? If you have every intention of becoming nurse, doctor, professor, instructor, teacher, or business CEO, then yes. But if you think you're gonna end up working in a fast food chain flipping burger or serving food, then a simple internship might be better for you, as college will only waste your time.

ESSAY ON WHY HIGH SCHOOL STUDENTS SHOULD HOLD PART TIME JOBS

What are the benefits of working a part time job in high school? After completing your homework each day, do you find yourself wasting the rest of the day watching TV or texting with your friends? If you find yourself with free time after completing your studies and other after school activities, you may want to consider obtaining a part-time job while you are in high school.

What are the benefits of working a part-time job while you are in high school? You will learn how to handle responsibility. Being a good student takes a lot of responsibility, but if you learn how to balance school studies/activities and a part-time job, you'll learn the true meaning of responsibility. As you grow older, your amount of responsibilities will only increase, so learning how to multitask at an early age will better prepare you for the future. You will show college admission offices that you are motivated to succeed. Most college admission offices like seeing work experience on a student's high school resume. To them, working a part-time job shows maturity and conscientiousness, which are qualities that are very important in a successful college student. Furthermore, if your part-time job is related to your intended major then college admission offices will see that you are a student who takes initiative and is focused on pursuing a successful career. You will discover how to manage your time more efficiently. With the decrease in free time that comes along with a part-time job, you will inevitably improve your time management skills. You will learn how to use your time more effectively, such as complete reading assignments during your bus ride home. By using a daily or an app on your smartphone to schedule your study time, extracurricular activities, work hours, etc., you will also learn the importance of becoming more organized.

You can explore career options before choosing your college major. By working different part-time jobs during your years in high school, you will more fully discern the type of career path you want to follow. If you find that you live working in a clothing store, maybe you would want to pursue a career in fashion. If you discover that you don't enjoy working part-time at your dad's office, perhaps you would consider a career path that focuses on outdoor activities.

By working various part-time jobs, you will learn what you are looking for and what you aren't looking for in a career. You will learn the importance of money management. When you start earning your own money, you will gain a better understanding of how to

handle it. Working hard for your own money will help you appreciate
important personal finance lessons such as benefits of budgeting,
and the importance of saving and being frugal.

In conclusion, while there are many benefits of having a part-time
job in high-school, not all students are capable of handling it
during the school year. If your high-school grades begin to suffer
or you aren't getting enough sleep, you should cut back on your work
hours (maximum of 10-15 hours per week) or working only during the
summer.

ESSAY ON THE LYMPHATIC SYSTEM

The lymphatic system is very important. It helps with the
cardiovascular and immune system. The lymphatic system is made up of
two semi-independent parts. One is a network of lymphatic vessels.
The other part is various lymphoid tissues and organs all over the
body. The functions of the lymphatic system include transporting
fluids that have escaped from the blood vascular system, and the
organ house phagocytic cells and lymphocytes. Lymphatic vessels are
an elaborate system of drainage vessels that collect the excess
protein-containing fluid and returns it to the bloodstream.

Once an intestial fluid enters the lymphatics it is called lymph.
The lymphatic vessels form a one way system in which lymph flows
only toward the heart. This entire transport system starts at the
lymph capillaries. These are very common, and usually occur in the
places blood capillaries occur. Lymph capillaries are not found in
bone, teeth, bone marrow, and entire central nervous system.

Lymphatic capillaries are very permeable. The endothelial cells that
make up the walls of the capillaries are not tightly joined.

Filament anchor the endothelium cells so they can expand. Pathogens can spread through the body through the lymphatic system.

There are many types of cells in the lymphoid tissue. One type is called lymphocytes, which are reffered to often as T or B cells. Plasma cells are antibody-producing offspring of B cells. Macrophages a phagocytes that help out with immunity. Reticular cells are cells that form the lymphoid tissue stoma. These cells are very important parts of the immune system.

The lymphatic system also contains tissues. The tissue of the lymphatic system is reticular connective tissue. It holds the macrophages and changes the number of lymphocytes. It is an important part of the immune system. The lymphoid tissue can be found in the follicles. Lymphoid organs are discrete and encapsulated. The main lymphoid organs are the spleen, tonsils, thymus, and lymph nodes.

The lymph nodes are placed along the lymphatic vessels. Each node has a fibrous capsule, a cortex, and a medulla. The lymph nodes help to circulate fluids. The lymph enters the lymph nodes through afferent lymphatic vessels and exits through the efferent vessels (afferent=enter, efferent=exit). Most lymphoid organs contain both macrophages and lymphocytes.

The spleen is an important place for immune function, and it kills defective or aged red blood cells and blood-borne pathogens. The spleen also stores platelets, products of hemoglobin, and acts as a hematopoietic site in the fetus.

The thymus contains hormones and is mostly functional in youth. Peyer's patches are on the tonsils, intestinal wall, lymphatic modules of the appendix and modules of the respiratory tract.

The many functions of the lymphatic system help the body maintain homeostasis. The many functions of removing foreign matter, and maintaining correct blood volume, are very important in immunity.

ESSAY ON ADVANTAGES AND DISADVANTAGES OF OWNING A BUSINESS

Businesses have been around since the time of the Roman Empire. They were trading for goods or selling handmade crafts such as pottery or clothes. Then as they conquered other countries, they brought the tradition of a business, such as a small family owned restaurant or market with them.

Then the Englishmen brought business with them. They started by trading with the Indians, then the English Crown decided to enforce the monetary system, using coins. There was still trade between the colonists, but those who didn't trade went to the market to buy the stuff that they needed.

But having a business has its advantages and disadvantages. An advantage of having a business is profits. If you are good and people like what you sell, then you can enjoy seeing your profits rise. Also another advantage of having a business is having the ability to mingle with the other society and make friends. Especially if you are retired and have enough money, opening a family business can come in good use. Opening a business also gives you a chance to prove that you are better than the other business people, like say for instance, a homeless person walks into your store or restaurant and asks for a bite to eat. Giving them a plate of food, a fruit to eat, or a little bit of money, won't hurt.

But owning a business has its disadvantages. Imagine opening a gas station and post signs all over the premises, "NO SMOKING". Then somebody who doesn't think gas is dangerous, or decides that signs don't mean anything, comes around to put gas, lights up a cigarette, not to mention that he lights himself up to, and then, poff,your gas station explodes into tiny bits of dust and cement, not to mention how much profits you'll also lose to rebuild you gas station. Many of the situations could happen. Now imagine you running peaceful errands in your store when all of a sudden a guy with a mask and a gun, comes to your cash register and tells you empty all your profits in his bag. Of course you don't have to do it, but unless you have something or somebody to protect you, you have no choice, unless you want him to kill or injure every body in your business.

So, in conclusion, if you have a business you should probably focus on proper security for your store. With proper security, and safety standards, you can ensure that you will have a successful business.

ESSAY ON AIRPLANES

What is an airplane? An airplane is a powered fixed-wing aircraft
that is propelled foward from thrust from a jet-engine, propeller,
or rocket. Airplanes have many uses in today's world. They are used
to transport cargo and people long distances. Some planes are used
for recreation. Planes also serve an important purpose in today's
military, as bombers, reconissance aircraft, stealth fighters, and
attack aircraft. This essay will provide a timeline of the first
successful aircraft flown, types of aircraft propulsion and the
advantages and disadvantages of aircraft.

The first aircraft ever successfully flown was built by the Wright
Brothers in 1903 in Kitty Hawk, North Carolina. After this, other
predecessors include the Brazalian Alberto Santos-Dumont, which in
1906 is claimed to be the first flight unassisted by a catapult.
Then came the Blériot VIII design of 1908, which had movable tail
surfaces controlling both yaw and pitch, a form of roll control
supplied either by wing warping or by ailerons, which controlled by
the controlled by the pilot.

Then came World War I, in which airpower became increasingly
important for reconissance. Since the Germans began using Zepplins
for reconissance and bombing raids, the importance of aircraft in
World War I was realized. The first succesful fighter aircraft was
the British Vickers
F. B. 5.

By World War II, aircraft had been modernized and improved, and were
used in all battles by all countries during the war. Also during the

war, both the United States and Japan had developed planes the
capable of operating from aircraft carriers.

Lastly, the first jet powered fighter aircraft was the German
Heinkel He 178, which was tested in 1939. The first commercially
used jet airliner is the de Havilland Comet, which was introduced in
1952, and used a Boeing 707, which was the first successful
commercial jet, in service for 50 years from 1958 to 2010.

How are aircraft powered? There are many ways that aircraft are
powered. There are three common ways aircraft air powered:
reciprocating engines, gas turbine (turboprop), and electric motor.
Reciprocating engine powered planes use an engine in which the
cylinders "radiate" outward from a central crankcase like the spokes
of a wheel and was commonly used for aircraft engines before gas
turbine engines became predominant. Gas engines, or commonly
reffered to as turboprop planes, have an intake, compressor,
combustor, turbine, and a propelling nozzel, which provide power
from a shaft through a reduction gear to the propeller. Last, but
not least, electric motor planes use power from solar cells,
ultracapacitors, or batteries. One example is the Solar Impulse 1, a
solar powered plane that runs on electric motors.

What are the advantages and disadvantages of airplanes? There are
many good uses for airplanes in the modern world. Airplanes can get
people and goods across oceans and forests faster than boats and
cars. Airplanes designed for military purposes can be used for
reconissance, military cargo transportation, fighter jets that can
operate from both land and sea (carrier based aircraft), and bomber
aircraft. Airplanes are also used for weather research. But there
are disadvantages to having airplanes. Most airplanes travel high in
the atmosphere, which eject large amounts of pollution, and
contribute to large amounts of greenhouse gases being thrown into
the atmosphere. Also, airplanes can be an easy target for
terrorists, looking to take hostage or kill large amounts of people.
One example was the 9/11 attack.

In conclusion, while planes have many good purpose in life, proper
safety measures must be taken to prevent planes from falling to the
wrong hands, and better, more efficient engines must be produced to
prevent our atmosphere from getting polluted.

ESSAY ON ELECTRICITY

In today's age of modern technology, electricity has become a
fundamental part of our life, from running desktop computers, to
electric trains, and soon the electric car. In this essay, we will

provide a comprehensive timeline of the first commercial generator, and break down the many different types of electricity, where they come from, and their advantages and disadvantages.

First, let us start with the timeline of the first commercial use of an electric generator. The first generator powerful enough to power large scale industry was built in early 1871 by Belgian inventor Zénobe Gramme. Then, in 1878 an hydroelectric power plant was built by William, Lord Armstrong at Cragside, England. It used water from lakes on his estate to power Siemens dynamos. The electricity supplied power to lights, heating, produced hot water, ran an elevator as well as labor-saving devices and farm buildings. By the autumn of 1881, a central station providing public power was built Godalming, England. It used hydroelectricity for street and household lighting. Although this wasn't very successful commercially and the town went back to using gas. Then, by 1882, the world's first coal powered electric plant was by Thomas Edison in London, before building the Pearl Street Station in September 1882 in New York. This station provided electric lighting in the lower Manhattan Island area. Due to the usage of DC (direct current) distribution, the service area was small, due to a voltage drop over long distances, that is, until the AC (alternating current) was developed in 1886 by George Westinghouse. It used a transformer to step up the electrical current for long distance transportation over power lines, then reduced the current for indoor electricity.

There are many different ways electricity can be produced. Coal, gas, nuclear power, hydroelectricity, geothermal electricity, wind energy, and solar power are all many ways that electricity can be produced. Electricity that is produced by using fossil fuels such as coal and gas are called thermal power plants. Fossil fuel power stations have machinery to convert the heat energy of combustion into mechanical energy, which then operates an electrical generator. Meanwhile, electricity that is produced by nuclear fusion is called nuclear power. A reactor produces a stable chemical reaction that creates heat for the steam needed to turn the turbines to produce electricity. Electricity that are produced by wind or solar power are called renewable energy, because they use natural resources that don't run out.

So which method is best to use as an electricity source? Thermal energy, nuclear energy, or renewable energy? Thermal energy, uses fossil fuels such as coal and gas to create heat. But power plants that use fossil fuels emit harmful CO2 gases that pollute the planet by creating smog, which is also a greenhouse gas that is bad for people to breath. Nuclear power plants are cleaner in many ways, but there are some drawbacks. If the nuclear power plant is located in an earthquake prone location, the earthquake can cause the reactor to fail, causing toxic radioactive gases to leak out, which is bad for the people. One example is the Fukoshima reactor failure during the 2011 earthquake in Japan. Plus, nuclear power is not exactly zero CO2 emissions, since the radioactive material, such as uranium, have to be mined from the earth, which, like coal, is mined using big excavator vehicles, which burn fuel and release CO2. Although

materials such as wind turbines, solar panels, and hydroelectric
dams have to be built, which in turn also releases CO2, they do not
release continous CO2, because once the plants are built, they start
producing clean energy, which makes up for the CO2 burnt. Overall,
nuclear and renewable energy can benefit the earth and the human
population more than thermal energy, while also conserving resources
such as coal and gas.

In conclusion, electrical usage has come very far since it was first
commercial produced. Now electricity is used for many different
purposes, and produced in many different ways, and if produced
wisely and cleanly, could be very beneficial to the human race.

ESSAY ON THE ENDOCRINE SYSTEM

What is the endocrine system? The endocrine system is a chemical
messenger system containing feedback loops of the hormones released
by the internal glands of an organism directly into the circulatory
system, regulating distant organs. The hypothalamus is the neural
control center for the endocrine system in vertebrates. The thyroid
gland and adrenal gland are the major endocrine glands in humans. In
addition to those glands, there are other organs in the body that
can perform secondary endocrine functions. These include: bone,
kidneys, liver, heart, and gonads. The kidneys secret the hormone
erythropoietin.

What are the major glands of the endocrine system? The major glands
of the endocrine system are: pineal gland, pituitary gland,
pancreas, ovaries, testes, thyroid gland, parathyroid gland,
hypothalamus and adrenal glands.

What role does the hypothalamus and anterior pituitary glands play
in the endocrine system? The hypothalamus regulates the autonomous
nervous system. The endocrine system has three sets of outputs: the
magnocellular system, the parvocellular system, and the autonomic
intervention. The anterior pituitary produces and secretes tropic
hormones such as: TSH, ACTH, GH, LH, and FSH.

What cells make up the endocrine system? The endocrine contains many
cells that usually form large tissues or organs. Here is a list with
some of their functions:

1. Hypothalamus

2. Anterior pituitary gland

3. Pineal gland

4. Posterior pituitary gland: this gland is part of the pituitary
    gland. It secretes hormones such as the antidiuretic hormone
    (ADH) and oxytocin. ADH helps the body to retain water, which is
    important in maintaining homeostatic balance between blood
    solutions and water. Oxytocin helps to induce uterine
    contractions and stimulate lactation.

5. Thyroid gland: the cells of the thyroid gland produce and
    secrete the T3 and T4 hormones in response to elevated levels of
    TRH, which are produced by the hypothalamus, and elevated levels
    of TSH, which are produced by the anterior pituitary gland,
    which regulates metabollic activity, including cell growth and
    tissue differentiation.

6. Parathyroid gland: cells of the parathyroid gland are richly
    supplied with blood from the inferior and superior thyroid
    arteries and secrete parathyroid hormone (PTH). PTH acts on
    bones, kidneys, and the GI tract to increase calcium
    reabsorption and phosphate excretion. PTH also helps with the
    conversion of Vitamin D into its most active form, 1,25-
    dihydroxyvitamin D3, which further helps in the absorption of
    calcium in the GI tract.

7. Adrenal glands (adrenal cortex & adrenal medulla)

8. Pancreas (alpha cells): these cells secrete hormones to help
    maintain homeostatic blood pressure. Insulin is also produced to
    lower blood sugar to normal levels, while glucagon is produced
    to activate glycogen stores in the liver to raise blood sugar to
    normal levels.

Also part of the pancreas
    Beta cells
    Delta cells
    F cells

9. Ovaries (granulosa cells)

10. Testis (leydig cells)

What are the functions of the hormones of the endocrine system? The
hormones of the endocrine system help with physiological and
behavioral activities such as: digestion, metabolism, respiration,
tissue function, sensory perception, sleep, excretion, lactation,
stress, growth and development, movement, reproduction, and mood.

What are the major defects that can happen if the endocrine system
malfunctions? There are a few major diseases that can happen due to
the malfunction of the endocrine system, including, diabetes
mellitus, thyroid disease, and obesity. Endocrine diseases can
happen due to misregulated hormone release (a productive pituitary
adenoma), inappropriate response to signaling (hypothyroidism), lack
of a gland (diabetes mellitus type 1, diminished erythropoiesis in
chronic kidney failure), or structural enlargement in a critical

site such as the thyroid (toxic multinodular goitre). Other common
diseases that can result from endocrine system dysfunction include:
Addison's disease, Cushing's disease and Graves' disease.

In conclusion, as outlined above, the endocrine system plays an
important role in the body's functions, and helps keeps the body
stable. It is therefore important to keep the endocrine system
healthy, like sleeping well, eating healthy foods, and keeping track
of your hormone levels through blood tests. By doing these, you can
prevent the endocrine system from malfunction and causing harmful
disease.

ESSAY ON THE MOBILE PHONE

What is a mobile phone? The first mobile phone, or the smartphone as
it is now called today, was first created in 1992. It's original
name was Simon Personal Communicator, made by IBM. It was the first
device that combined the use of a regular phone with the use of a
PDA, a hand held device used to send emails and fax.

Today, there are many large smartphone manufacturers, like Apple and
Android. The first modern smartphone was created by Android in 2003,
and then bought by Google in 2005. Apple came out with its first
iPhone 2007. Since then, the smartphone has continued to evolve and
become more useful than just the normal phone.

You may ask yourself, "In what way are smartphones useful?"
Smartphones are useful in many ways. Smartphones have gps, and
online maps readily available for whenever the need arises, and you
can usually download directions to have them when you are offline.
Smartphones also come with the ability to listen to music you want
to listen, especially with earphones that you can plug into your
phone and listen personally, in case you don't like what the other
person is listening. Smartphones also give you the ability to email
or chat to your friends on the go, without losing contact.
Smartphones are also more compact than laptops, so you can carry
them where ever you may need them.

But there are many disadvantages of owning a smartphone. Many people get distracted while driving and texting at the same time, and car accidents tend to occur more frequently. Schoolchildren tend to carry smartphones to school, and their grades end up falling due to lack of concentration. Some smartphones, although they are continuously being improved, contain harmful radiation that can damage the eyes and brain.

How do we solve these problems? People, especially those who have important jobs, or own businesses, constantly have to keep in touch with their coworkers or boss, whether they are driving or not. But schoolchildren, have a more important goal of getting good grades to eventually succeed in life, and cannot afford to be texting their friends or playing video games while they are in class. How can we solve this issue? Require students to hand out their smartphones to the principal, where the principal can store them in a safe place until recess hours arrive. That way, students aren't constantly distracted by the buzzing of their friends text messages, or an interesting video game.

In conclusion, the smartphone is a good and useful invention, but if overused, can be harmful to kids and adults alike.

ESSAY ON THE IMMUNE SYSTEM

When a bacterium or virus invades the body, the white blood cells go into action, attacking foreign microorganisms in the blood, lymph and tissues.

Some white blood cells also produce antibodies. An antibody is a kind of secret weapon specially designed to detect a specific virus or bacterium. Each kind of bacterium or virus has its own distinctive chemical label called an antigen. Once the immune system determines the chemical identity of a specific virus or bacterium, white blood cells build a unique antibody to help neutralize the invader.

The antibody works by attaching itself to a specific location on the antigen and then disabling the virus or bacterium.

The antibody and antigen fit together like a lock and key. Once they are locked together, the invader is deactivated and loses its ability to cause harm.

After the antigen have been deactivated and the disease has been overcome, the antibodies that were made to attack that disease remain in the blood. If the same invader appears in the future, the antibodies already in the body can immediately attack the invading microbes and keep them from causing a disease or infection. Some antibodies can protect you from getting the same disease twice. For example, if you had the chicken pox, you will not get it again, because your body has built up a lifetime immunity. We say you are immune to chicken pox.

Unfortunately, there are some diseases that you can get again and again. An example of these is the flu. The reason your immune system cannot protect you from multiple cases of the flu is because the viruses that cause the flu are constantly changing. Each new version is a little different from the previous version, so the antibody the body developed last time you had the flu will probably not be effective against the new antigen. That means you will be sick with the flu until your body makes enough white blood cells with the antibodies to destroy the new viruses.

A human body needs a guardian that protects it from numerous harmful influences of the environment. The immune system plays the role of such a guardian. The word "immune" means "untouched" or 'free' from something. This is the most complex system in the human body that consists of different organs, the nervous system, proteins and cells. All the system components work together and their smooth work help people stay healthy and resist pathogens, e.g. a bacterium, virus, or other microorganisms that can cause a disease. However, sometimes the immune system cannot help, for instance, in case of an aggressive pathogen or the one that the body did not have contact previously.

The immune system performs the functions of neutralizing viruses, bacteria, and fungi, it recognizes potentially harmful substances that get inside the body from the environment, and provides support necessary to fight somehow changed cells, e.g. cancerous cells. The ability of the immune system to recognize 'self' and 'non-self' substances ensures effective protection of the organism. The former are called antigens, they are the proteins of pathogens. The defensive cells can be detected by these proteins and cause a series of specific processes in the cells. However, sometimes the system fails and identifies the 'self cells' as 'non self', so an autoimmune reaction takes place. The outstanding fact is that the human body 'remembers' which proteins are dangerous. There are 2 parts of the immune system, called the innate and adaptive. The innate immune system is responsible of the defense against non-specific pathogens, especially different bacteria. Genetic factors influence the human immune system, they play a vital role and protect infants until their adaptive immune system becomes well developed. Human genes define the number of major histocompatibility complex molecules that the cells carry. Some of them are believed to deal with the autoimmune diseases.

The adaptive immune system creates antibodies, special agents that are learnt to respond in a special way. It is developed after the organism has overcome a certain disease. In the future, the immune system will respond faster and more efficiently. Therefore, the human body can adapt and learn new things. However, both systems work together and complement to each other. For example, immunization helps the cells to recognize pathogens and fight them more efficiently.

In conclusion immune system should be able to function properly in order to maintain an overall health. People should avoid stress, have a balanced diet, get enough sleep, do sports and drop smoking. Therefore they will not weaken their immune system and live a long and healthier life.

ESSAY ON COMMUNICABLE DISEASES

Communicable diseases, also known as infectious diseases or
transmissible diseases, are illnesses that result from the
infection, presence and growth of pathogenic (capable of causing
disease) biologic agents in an individual human or other animal
host. Infections may range in severity from asymptomatic (without
symptoms) to severe and fatal. The term infection does not have the
same meaning as infectious disease because some infections do not
cause illness in host. Disease causing biologic agents include
viruses, bacteria, fungi, protozoa, muticellular parasites, and
aberrant proteins known as prions. Transmission of these biologic
agents can occur in a variety of ways, including direct physical
contact with an infectious person, consuming contaminated foods or
beverages, contacts with contaminated body fluids, contact with
contaminated inanimate objects, airbone (inhalation), or being
bitten by an infected insect or tick. Some disease agent can be
transmitted in more than one way. This essay will provide a list of
communicable diseases.

Signs and symptoms of tuberculosis: a bad cough that lasts 3 weeks
or longer, pain in the chest, coughing up blood or sputum (phlegm
from deep inside the lungs), weakness or fatigue, weight loss, no
appetite, chills, and fever. Causes of tuberculosis is by bacteria
that spread from person to person through microscopic droplets
released into the air. This can happen when someone with the
untreated, active form of tuberculosis coughs, speaks sneezes,
spits, laughs or sings. Although tuberculosis is contagious, it's
not easy to catch. You're more likely to get tuberculosis from
someone you live or work with than from a stranger. Most people
with active TB who've had appropriate drug treatment for at least 2
weeks are no longer contagious.

Prevention of tuberculosis. If you test positive for latent TB
infection, your doctor may advise you to take medications to reduce
your risk of developing active tuberculosis. The only type of type
of tuberculosis that is contagious is the active variety, when it
affects the lungs. So if you can prevent you latent tuberculosis
from becoming active, you won't transmit your tuberculosis to anyone
else.

Signs and symptoms of measles: a high temperature, sore eyes
(conjunctives), and runny nose usually occur first. Small white
spots usually develop inside the mouth a day or so later. A harsh
dry cough is usual. Going off food, tiredness, and aches and pains

are usual. Measles is caused by a virus. It is spread when an infected person coughs,sneezes, or shares food or drinks. The measles virus can travel through air. This means that you can get measles if you are near someone who has the virus even if that person doesn't cough or sneeze directly on you.

How to prevent measles? Measles vaccination has markedly reduced the number of incidence of measles throughout the developed world. However, measles cases still occur in undeveloped countries, since a single imported case can result in large measles outbreaks in the setting of waning immunity.

Signs and symptoms chicken pox: fever (temperature), aches and headaches often start a day or so before a rash appears. Rash. Spots appear in crops. They develop into small blister and are itchy. They can be anywhere on the body. Several crops may develop over several days. . . . Dry cough and sore throat are common. Chicken pox is caused by the varicella-zoster virus. It's a very contagious infection. About 90% of people who have not previously had chicken pox will come into contact with the virus.

Prevention of chicken pox (varicella) vaccine is the best way to prevent chicken pox.

Signs and symptoms of thypoid fever: fever that can reach as high as 104 degrees F (40 degrees C). Feeling achy, tired or weak, constipation, diarrhea, headache, stomach pain and loss of appetite and sore throat. Causes of thypoid fever is an acute illness associated with fever caused by the Salmonella paratyphi, a related bacterium that usually causes a less severe illness. The bacteria are deposited in water or food by a human carrier and are then spread to other people in the area.

Preventing thypoid fever is to get vaccinated against the illness. Two vaccines are available. A shot that contains killed Salmonella typhi bacteria and a vaccine taken by mouth containing a live but weakened strain of the bacteria. Avoiding risky foods and beverages (especially when traveling in the developing world) is another way to reduce your risk.

Signs and symptoms of mumps: fever, headache, muscle aches, tiredness, loss of appetite, swollen and tender salivary under the ears on one or both sides. Causes of mumps is by a virus called the paramyxovirus. It's spread from one child to another through direct contact with discharge from the nose and throat. Infected droplets in the air from a sneeze or close conversation can be inhaled, and may cause infection.

Prevention includes use of the mumps vaccine (administered in measles - mumps - rubella [MMR] or measles - mumps - rubella - varicella [MMRV] vaccines) is the best way to prevent mumps. Children should be given the first doses of mumps vaccine soon after their first birthday (12 to 15 months of age).

Signs and symptoms of hepatitis: fatigue, flu-like symptoms, dark urine, pale colored stool, abdominal pain, loss of appetite, unexplained weight loss, yellow skin and eyes (may be signs of jaundice). Hepatitis can be caused by liver damaged from excessive alcohol consumption. This is sometimes referred to as "alcohol hepatitis." The alcohol causes the liver to swell and become inflamed. Other toxic causes include overuse of medication or exposure to poison.

The hepatitis A vaccine can prevent infection with the virus. The hepatitis A vaccine is typically given in two doses-initial vaccination followed by a booster shot six months later. The Centers for Diseases and Prevention recommends the following individuals receive a hepatitis A vaccine.

Signs and symtoms of malaria: fever, chills, headache, sweats, fatigue, nausea, and vomiting. Malaria is caused by the plasmodium, the parasite that can be spread to humans through the bites of infected mosquitos.

Malaria can often be avoided using the ABCD approach to prevention which stands for: Awareness of risk-find out whether you are at risk of getting malaria. Bite-prevention-avoid mosquito bites by using insect repelent and using mosquito nets. Check whether you need to take malaria prevention tablets-if you do, make sure you take the right antimalarial tablets at the right dose, and finish the course. Diagnosis- seek immediate medical advice if you have malaria symptoms, including up to a year after you return from traveling.

Signs and symtoms of whooping cough: running nose, sneezing, mild cough, low grade fever. Causes of whooping cough is by infection with a bacterium known as Bordetella pertussis. The bacteria attach to the upper airways in the upper respiratory system and release toxins that lead to inflammation and swelling.

In the U.K. whooping cough is now rare due to the successful vaccination against it. The 5-in-1 vaccine. The whooping cough vaccine is given as part of the 5-in-1 vaccine (DTaP/IPV/HiB), which also protects against diptheria, tetanus, polio, and HiB (heamaphilus influenza type B).

Signs and symtoms of flu: a 100 degree F or higher fever or feeling feverish (not everyone with the flu has a fever). A cough and or sore throat. A runny or stuffy nose, headaches, and or body aches, chills, fatigue. The flu is actually very different from a cold. While more than 100 different viruses can cause a cold, only influenze type A, B, and C causes the flu. Type A and B viruses are responsible for the large flu epidemics. Type C flu virus is stable and usually causes milder respiratory systems.

If you are healthy but exposed to a person with the flu, antiviral drugs prevent you from getting sick. The sooner you are treated with the antiviral, the more likely it will prevent the flu. Antiviral drugs are 70% to 90% effective at preventing the flu.

Signs and symptoms of the common cold: sore throat, mucus build up
in the nose, difficulty breathing through your nose, swelling of
your sinuses, sneezing, cough, headache and tiredness. The common
cold is a self limited contagious illness that can be caused by a
number of different types of viruses. The common cold is medically
reffered to as a viral upper respiratory tract infection.

Preventing the common cold: no vaccine has been developed for the
common cold. But you can take some common-sense precautions to slow
the spread of the virus.

Now that you know the top 10 most contagious diseases, you can take
precautions on protecting yourself and your family from them and
keep them healthy.

ESSAY ON NON COMMUNICABLE DISEASES

A non-communicable disease (NCO) is a medical condition or disease
that is not caused by infectious agents (non-infectious or non-
transmissible). NCDs can refer to chronic diseases which last for
long periods of time and progress slowly. Sometimes, NCDs result in
rapid deaths such as seen in certain diseases such as autoimmune
diseases, heart diseases, stroke, cancers, diabetes, chronic kidney
disease, osteoporosis, Alzheimer's disease, cataracts, and others.

While sometimes referred to as synonymous with "chronic diseases",
NCDs are distinguished only by their duration, though some chronic
diseases of long duration maybe caused by infections. Chronic
diseases require chronic case management, as do all diseases that
are slow to develop and of long duration. NCDs are the leading cause
of death globally. About half are under the age of 70 and half were
women. Risk factors such as a person's background, lifestyle and
environment increase the likelihood of certain NCDs. Every year, at
least five million people die because of tobacco use and about 2.8
million die from being overweight. High cholesterol accounts for
roughly 2.6 million deaths and 7.5 million die because of high blood
pressure.

Risk factors such as a person's background, lifestyle and
environment are known to increase the likelihood of certain non
communicable diseases. They include age, gender, genetics, exposure
to air pollution, and behaviors such as smoking, unhealthy diet and
physical activity which can lead to hypertension and obesity in turn
leading to high risk of many NCDs. Most NCDs are considered
preventable because they are caused by modifiable risk factor.

The WHO's World Health Report in 2002 identified 5 important risk
factors for non-communicable disease in the top ten leading risks to
health. These are raised blood pressure, raised cholesterol, tobacco
use, alcohol consumption, and being overweight. The other factors
associated with higher risk of NCDs include a person's economic and
social conditions, also known as the "[social determination of
health]". It has been estimated that if the primary risks factors
were eliminated, 80% of the cases of health diseases, stroke, and
type 2 diabetes and 40% of cancers could be prevented. Interventions
targeting the main risk factors could have significant impact on
reducing th burden of disease worldwide. Efforts focused on better
diet and increased physical activity have been shown to control the
prevalence of NCDs.

ESSAY ON THE URINARY SYSTEM

The urinary system is a very important function of the human body.
The main parts of the human urinary system are the kidneys, ureter,
bladder and urethra.

How does the urinary system do all this? The formation of urine
starts in the kidneys, at the nephrons, which then pass through
collecting ducts. The collecting ducts then merge together to form
the minor calyces which are then followed by the major calyces that
join at the renal pelvis. The urine then travels from the renal
pelvis through the ureter, before being transported to the urinary
bladder.

What are the main functions of the urinary system? The urinary
system helps to regulate blood composition (sodium, potassium, and
calcium), regulate blood pressure, regulate blood homeostasis,
contributes to the production of red blood cells by the kidney,
helps synthesize calcitriol (the active form of Vitamin D), and
stores waste products (mainly urea and uric acid) before it and
other products are removed from the body.

How is urine formed? The first step in urine production is the
amount of blood that is being filtered. The kidney typically filters
1.25 L/min. The chief function of the kidney's nephron is to
regulate the concentration of water and solube substances like
sodium by filtering the blood, reabsorbing what is needed and
excreting the rest as urine. Depending on hydration and physical
activity, a healthy human produces about 1 to 2 liters of urine
daily. Polyuria is excessive urine production, oliguria is when <400
ml of urine is produced, and anuria is when <100 ml is produced.

What hormones influence the urinary system? The endocrine system
influences the urinary system through the hormones aldosterone,
antidiuretic hormone, and the parathyroid hormone. Aldosterone plays
a role in regulating blood pressure through its effects on the
kidney. It acts on the distal tubules and collecting ducts of the
nephrons and enhances reabsorption of sodium from the glomerular
filtrate. Reabsorption of sodium helps to retain water which
increases blood pressure and blood volume. Antidiuretic hormone

(ADH), is a neurohypophysial hormone found in most mammals. It helps
to retain water and permits vasoconstriction. Vasopressin helps in
the body's retention of water by increasing the kidney's water
permeability in its collecting ducts.

What are some of the malfunctions and diseases that can occur in the
urinary system? One is urinary tract obstruction that can cause
urinary retention. Others include bladder cancer, kidney cancer,
ureteral cancer, and urethral cancer. People who are trained to deal
with urinary tract complications are nephrologists and urologists.
Gynecologists can help with female urinary tract complications.

In conclusion, maintaining a healthy urinary system can help the
urinary system maintain normal bodily functions such as maintaining
blood ph and normal blood volume.

ESSAY ON VOLCANOES

Volcanoes have many beneficial uses. They help cleanse the planet of
old and dying living things like plants, and replace them with new
growth. They create fertile land for the farmers to grow crops. Lava
flows from these volcanoes going to the ocean like, for instance,
K?lauea, in Hawaii, can lead to the formation of new islands for
people to live on, or for plants and animals to find new life.
Volcanoes, under special precuations and safety regulations, can
also serve as tourist spots for people and residents alike to see a
volcano upclose.

But volcanoes are very dangerous. People have become so intimidated
by a volcano's beauty and magnificent scenery that they have
developed ways of building massive cities close to a volcano, which
in turn, creates a humanitarian hazard when the volcano erupts,

causing the deaths of many people. Although these cities have early warning systems that can warn the people days or even weeks before a volcanic eruption, some people may chose to ignore these warnings until the last minute, or they may never evacuate. This happened with the eruption of Mount Saint Helens on May 22,1980 when 57 people on and around the volcano died.

In conclusion, volcanoes have their uses in promoting the growth of new life by removing old life, and volcanoes can serve as tourist attractions, like the K?lauea volcano in Hawaii, and St.Helens in Washington, but cities shouldn't be built so close to a volcano. State and local governments should create hazard zones in which no residential or commercial building should be built within a certain radius of the volcano. Doing this can help to ensure that people who chose to live close to a volcano, can have some safety.

www.ingramcontent.com/pod-product-compliance
Lightning Source LLC
Chambersburg PA
CBHW080851160726
47999CB00009B/3082